A WALK AROUND ISRAEL

A Walk Around Israel

Scriptures taken from the Holy Bible, New International Version, NIV, Copyright 1973, 1978, 1984, 2011 by Biblica, Inc. Used by permission of Zondervan. All rights reserved worldwide. www.zondervan.com The "NIV" and "New International Version" are trademarks registered in the United States Patent and Trademark Office by Biblica, Inc.

For information contact: Shalako Press, 414 Shalako Drive, Oakdale, CA 95361

ISBN   979-8-9861870-0-6

A WALK AROUND ISRAEL

By Leslie A. Sousa

Illustrations by Ellen Herod

Shalako Press

INTRODUCTION

Walk down the Via Delarosa
Float in the Dead Sea
Sit in the Praetorium
Walk Around Israel with me.

Reach high up on the Wailing Wall
Pick up stones in Elah Valley
Walk down the Southern Steps
Kneel in the Garden of Gethsemane.

Take in the clear, cool waters of Ein Gedi
Where we splashed uninhibited
The Sea of Galilee, Beit She'an,
The Garden Tomb
Some of the amazing places that we visited.

Sit beside the Pool of Bethesda
See Jesus's power at the Pool of Siloam
Look over Bethlehem, the neighboring Shepherds' Field
The Valley of Armageddon.

Pick up seashells on the shores of Caesarea
Take a cable car ride to Masada
Stand outside the entrance of Yad Vashem
Overlook the Mediterranean Sea in Joppa.

Learn from Pastor Damian's themes
Know the God of second chances
Grow in your relationship with the King
Or begin one of life's greatest romances.

Be reminded that our failure
Will never have the final say
To put no one in the "never category"
Be confident in the same God of yesterday.

Study the recipe of a blessed life
Be assured He will never let you go
Understand the end of the story
It is the most important part to know.

Become aware of how far-reaching
Just one decision against God can be
Don't be like the man of excuses
Realize the power of your testimony.

Admire Vic's Armenian Art Studio
Consider trying a falafel
Be served a whole St. Peter's Fish
Know the meaning behind the tear bottle.

Walk around Israel with me
By the time that we are through
My hope is that you will know
Just how much God loves you!

For God so loved the world that he gave his one and only Son, that whoever believes in him shall
not perish but have eternal life. - John 3:16

For Annie

She had a great eye for color
Loved the fall season and art
Was spunky, loved to wrestle
A real tomboy at heart.

Introverted, introspective
Reserved, slow to speak
She loved profoundly
Was thoughtful and meek.

No time for superficial friendships
Bowing humbly to lift
The needs of her intimate friends
In prayer, was her gift.

Thoughtful, meditative
Longed for relationships deep
Lover of orange, brown, and yellow
A huge dimple in her cheek.

On the trip of a lifetime
Where the Bible comes to life
I had the pleasure of meeting
Christian and his wife.

Asked the highlight of our trip
She and I answered the same
It was being baptized in the Jordan River
In the Father, Son, and Holy Spirit's name.

Written in Hebrew on her finger
A reminder not to fear
Was Isaiah 41:10
Her greatest souvenir.

Ellen soon joined us
I call her *God's easel*
You can see through her watercolors
All the beauties of Israel.

Through spiritual unity and fellowship
We became the "Christian buds"
We laughed when we shortened it
And we became the "cruds."

She found solace by the ocean
Pacific Grove she visited often
The time God gave me with her
Will never be forgotten.

"So do not fear, for I am with you;
Do not be dismayed, for I am your
God. I will strengthen you and
help you; I will uphold you with
My righteous right hand." Isaiah 41:10

A WALK AROUND ISRAEL

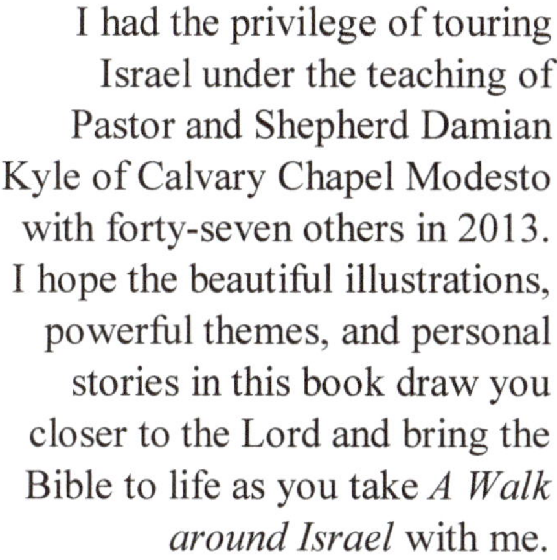

Our Annie (left)

I had the privilege of touring Israel under the teaching of Pastor and Shepherd Damian Kyle of Calvary Chapel Modesto with forty-seven others in 2013. I hope the beautiful illustrations, powerful themes, and personal stories in this book draw you closer to the Lord and bring the Bible to life as you take *A Walk around Israel* with me.

Leslie Sousa (center)

I started sketching and doing watercolor postcards on my first trip to Israel in 2000. At each site Pastor Damian taught, I'd do a quick sketch and copy them on watercolor paper in the evening to make postcards to give to family and friends. This book is an accumulation of many of those images. Thank you to Lucy Abbey, who has been such an encouragement and has scanned and kept a digital file of them for me. *A Walk Around Israel* is a sweet reminder of the places I've visited in Israel, the people I met, and the lessons I learned about myself and Jesus.

Ellen Herod (right)

Annie, Leslie & Ellen 2013

The journey begins . . .

Caesarea

The first place we visited was Caesarea, where we took turns reading Acts, Chapter 26, and sang one of my mom's favorite songs, "How Great Thou Art." The theme was ***TESTIMONY.*** Remember the miracle of your testimony, what you were, how you came to know Christ, and what you are becoming now. Thank God for "your story." Like a fingerprint, no two are alike.

Caesarea

We didn't have teaching at this site, but I heard something interesting. Herod built the Roman Aqueduct to bring fresh water from Mount Carmel to Caesarea. The water had to travel some twenty-three miles to reach the men, and by that time, it was lukewarm, so they would spit it out. Likewise, in Revelation 3:15-16, "I know your deeds, that you are neither cold nor hot. I wish you were either one or the other! So, because you are lukewarm-neither hot nor cold-I am about to spit you out of my mouth." Be hot and healing or cold and refreshing.

Our next stop was Mount Carmel, where we took turns reading 1 Kings 18:1-40. The theme was ***WHOLEHEARTEDNESS***. When God calls us, we should be immediately obedient with our whole heart, even if it means He has to change someone else's heart that appears to us unchangeable. He will be faithful. If we give God anything less than our *whole* heart, we will never be *whole* spiritually.

After eating Israel's national snack called a Falafel, I jokingly named the deep-fried ball made from ground chickpeas, the "feel-awful." It was delicious! But it will always be the "feel-awful" to me.

At Megiddo, Valley of Armageddon, we took turns reading Revelation 19:11-20:6. The theme was **PEACE**. Know the end of the story. *God wins*!

He let us know the end of the story so that we can walk through life in His peace.

Our bus driver pulled over, and we all got out at a place that overlooked Nazareth, the home of Joseph, Mary, and Jesus. It was here Jesus spent His childhood, taught in the synagogue, and was rejected, "Truly I tell you," He continued, "no prophet is accepted in his hometown." We took turns reading Luke 4:16-30. The theme was **REJECTION**. Rejection is the most painful emotion, especially when it comes from your own friends and family.

It was also here, in Luke 1:12-38, that the angel told Mary she had found favor with God, and she would conceive and give birth to a son she was to call Jesus. Mary answered, "I am the Lord's servant. May your word to me be fulfilled." The theme was **SURRENDER**. This is one of Karin Kyle's favorite verses.

"The main reason for Jesus's miracles was to demonstrate that God was with Him, and that He was the promised Savior sent from God. "– Billy Graham

In John 2:1-11, Jesus performed the first miracle in His public ministry by turning water into wine. Jesus, His mother Mary, and His disciples were among the guests at the Wedding Feast in Cana when, on the third day of festivities, the wine ran out. Mary tells the servants to do whatever Jesus says. We are also Jesus's servants and should do the same.

He gives us insurmountable grace. He changes hearts. He forgives our sins. Our God is the God of miracles.

On the Road to Damascus, we took turns reading Acts 9:1-22. Saul vehemently opposed spreading the gospel and he had every intention of continuing his vicious plans against Christians as he walked down this road. But a light came down from heaven, "I am Jesus, whom you are persecuting." Here Saul was converted to Christianity, blinded, and had his name changed to Paul. Paul was the last person anyone would have thought could be saved. The theme was **CONVERSION**. No one is hopeless. Never put anyone in the "never" category.

My sweetest memory on the Road to Damascus was the one and only time we held hands. If we were comfortable doing so, we were encouraged to pray aloud for our friends and loved ones who were heaviest on our hearts that day. When I opened my eyes, I saw a perfect heart-shaped rock, so I gave it a new home on my desk at work. It serves as a daily reminder that God holds our right hand and says to us, "Do not fear. I will help you." Isaiah 41:13

The 13th-century remains of Nimrod Fortress sit upon a hill that features picturesque views. The remnants are part of a national park that sits close to Israel's highest and only snowcapped mountain, Mount Hermon. It is the largest castle from the Crusade era and is a kid-friendly tourist attraction.

On top of Mount Arbel, we saw a replica of the basket used by the Roman soldiers to lower themselves down the mountain in search of Jews. When they found one, they would pull them from the safety of the cave to their death in the valley below by using a sizeable hook-like instrument.

Jesus leads three of His disciples "up to a high mountain" and appears before them changed. "His face shone like the sun, and His clothes became as white as the light." Matthew 17:1 It is widely believed that the Transfiguration of Jesus took place in the Mount Hermon area.

Mount Hermon is on the border between Syria and Lebanon. Two-thirds of the year, its peak is covered with snow. There is hardly any soil or vegetation above the snowline but there are vineyards, trees, and wildlife below.

In Caesarea Philippi, we took turns reading Matthew 16:13-20. The critical question is found in verse 15, "But who do *you* say that I am?" Lord, Liar or Lunatic - C.S. Lewis. Here Peter confesses that Jesus is Lord. The theme was ***CONFESSION***. Jesus describes the person who comes to the proper conclusion of who He is and confesses Him to be "the Christ, the Son of the living God" as *blessed*.

After hiking a beautiful trail to the city gate at Tel Dan, we took turns reading 1 Kings 12:25-33. The theme was **_DECISIONS_**, just how far-reaching one decision against God can be.

We all leave a legacy determined by our decisions, no matter how small a position we are in. Ask yourself, "Does this decision glorify God? Is this decision in obedience to God's Word?" If your answer is yes, you can walk in peace knowing your decision is good and will leave a Godly legacy.

From a boat on the Sea of Galilee, we took turns reading Mark 4:35-5:1. We talked about the levels of trials; challenging, more complex, and the ones where we ask God, "Where are you?" The theme here was ***CONFIDENCE***, and we sang the song, "You Never Let Go."

He won't let us sink as long as we keep our eyes on Him. He is our "Good, Good Father," just like the song by Chris Tomlin. One we can both love and fear (be in respect and awe of). If we fear the Lord, we have nothing else to fear.

The Jesus Boat Exhibit houses an old fishing vessel discovered in 1986 on the shore of the Sea of Galilee. The boat precedes the 1st century AD. An incredible story of the discovery of the boat, its excavation, and conservation plays as you examine the boat. The DVD is available for purchase at the exhibit. It was here that I also bought a beautifully embroidered prayer shawl.

When seven of the disciples were having a hard time making a catch after a whole night of fishing, Jesus told Simon Peter to cast his net out to the other side of the boat. When he did as Jesus instructed him to do, there was an overabundance of fish caught, so much so that the net almost burst open. That is when Jesus told the fishermen to become "fishers of men."

Fortunately, we can still enjoy a St. Peter's Fish today. (Pictured at the Tanureen restaurant.)

The Mount of Beatitudes is the title given to the place where Jesus delivered His Sermon on the Mount—the recipe for a blessed life. Here we took turns reading Matthew, Chapter 5. The theme was ***BLESSING***. God calls us to be the salt of the earth and the light of the world, so shine bright!

What is the recipe for a blessed life?

Poor in Spirit: humility
Mourning: engaged in humankind
Meek: gentleness and a thirst for God
Mercy: people make mistakes
Pure: a clean heart
Peacemaker: an instrument of peace
Persecuted: for righteousness's sake

Mount of Beatitudes

It was here in Capernaum where Jesus performed many of His miracles including healing the man with the withered hand. We took turns reading Mark, Chapter 3. The theme was *ABILITY*. We protect our withered areas with excuses, but Jesus never gives us a command without giving us His power to fulfill it. We will never access that power until we take the first step to obey the commandment. Whether we take the first step to obey or not determines whether our withered areas will be healed.

Jesus's attention always went to the person with the greatest need in the room. Look for the person with the greatest need, not the most convenient one.

At Tabgha, the traditional site of the multiplication, Jesus' feeding of the 5,000 with the five loaves and two fish, we took turns reading John, Chapter 21. The steps here are the original steps but the church was built later. The theme was **RESTORATION**. God will not allow a failure to have the final say in our life.

Find encouragement in 1 and 2 Peter. Longevity in the Lord and how we respond when we fail are key. God restored Peter's failure to be a trophy of his faith. If Peter had never failed, he would not have been a carrier of God's grace. Jesus prayed Peter's *faith* would not fail, not that *he* wouldn't fail. Remember God's Word is the same today. Allow God's grace to have the final say in your life.

For the Lord your God is bringing you into a good land—a land with brooks, streams, and deep springs gushing out into the valleys and hills; a land with wheat and barley, vines and fig trees, pomegranates, olive oil and honey. Deuteronomy 8:7-8

They made the robe of the ephod entirely of blue cloth—the work of a weaver—with an opening in the center of the robe like the opening of a collar, and a band around this opening, so that it would not tear. They made pomegranates of blue, purple and scarlet yarn, and finely twisted linen around the hem of the robe. And they made bells of pure gold and attached them around the hem between the pomegranates. The bells and pomegranates alternated around the hem of the robe to be worn for ministering, as the Lord commanded Moses. Exodus 39:22-26

Gadara was where Jesus delivered the demoniac from a Legion of demons. When the Legion of demons left the man, they went into a herd of swine, over a cliff, and drowned. In this area, we took turns reading Mark, Chapter 5. The theme was the ***POWER OF JESUS***.

At Beit She'an, we took turns reading 1 Samuel, Chapter 31. Saul was called by God, anointed by God, handsome, kind, and good. He had unlimited potential, but he ended his life in complete failure. He is "the man who never repented." It was always someone else's fault. The theme here was **EXCUSES**. Like a half-truth is a whole lie, partial obedience is complete disobedience.

Our next stop was Gideon Springs, where we took turns reading Judges 7:1-7, 19-25. It was here Gideon chose the three hundred men who would fight the Midianites by the way they drank water. The theme was **TESTING** and the test was based on how the men conducted themselves in an ordinary event of life. Is there anything more ordinary than getting a drink of water?

God chose men who, even though they were busy with their ordinary lives, stayed engaged, watchful, clearheaded, alert, and on duty. Almost all of us can do that for a little while but to do that daily indicates those qualities have become a part of our character. How we handle the ordinary in life reveals more about us than how we handle the extraordinary.

The Dead Sea is located between Israel and Jordan. It is dense, and the salt content is very high making it almost impossible to swim. The Dead Sea has the lowest elevation on the earth's surface, and there is no life in its waters.

In Ezekiel 47:1-12, the prophet tells us an incredible vision of a stream of water coming down from the Temple of Jerusalem. It sweeps down to the Dead Sea and heals the waters making the sea full of fish. This vision will occur during Jesus' Millennial Kingdom!

My roommate and I floated on the Dead Sea under a full moon and a sky full of stars. Truly amazing!

The Zealots had agreed long before the impending attack of the Romans to serve God and not any other master. Here at Masada, Elazar Ben-Yair, the leader of the Zealots, called his people together and convinced them to commit suicide rather than surrender the fortress. Before the morning attack, they burned their belongings and weapons. They left food so the Romans would know they had not died from hunger but of their own free will. The Zealots cast lots to choose ten men to kill the others. They then chose one man among the ten who would kill the nine survivors. That last man then killed himself.

You can take the tram or the 700 stair Snake Path up to Masada. I took the tram up and the stairs down, followed by drinking a new favorite pink grapefruit drink I found in Israel. You can't find them everywhere in Israel, but I recommend you keep your eye out for one if you are ever there.

God gives us the calling. Then He provides us with the vision. Then He "prepares" us for something extraordinary. At Ein Gedi, a central oasis along the western side of the Dead Sea, we took turns reading 1 Samuel, Chapter 24. Ein Gedi is known principally for being one of David's hiding places while fleeing King Saul. It is full of rocks and caves, making it an excellent place for hiding and refuge. The theme here was **PREPARATION**. Psalm 57 is David's perspective during his preparation. Don't ever forget something good is coming.

The Jericho Road was the Roman road used at the time of Jesus to travel back and forth between Jericho and Jerusalem. It was the road that Jesus referred to in His story of *The Good Samaritan*. Here we took turns reading Luke 10:25-37. It is Jesus's answer to, "Who is my neighbor?" "You shall love the Lord your God with all your heart and with all your soul and with all your strength and with all your mind, and your neighbor as yourself." The most important eighteen inches is from your head to your heart. The theme was ***DOING***.

I always wanted to ride a camel, and I was touched when our tour guide made the arrangements for our group to do so. The camel I had the pleasure of riding was named Kojak. I would describe him as cute, although I'm not sure how anyone else would describe a camel. He even smiled at the camera! I was surprised by how tall he was and even more so by how high up I was after I got on him. I would do it again in a heartbeat!

As we entered *The Holy City* of Jerusalem, we sang a song by the same name to the top of our lungs, proudly and fervently.

> "Jerusalem! Jerusalem!
> Lift up your gates and sing,
> Hosanna in the highest!
> Hosanna to your King!"

At the Mount of Olives, overlooking the Kidron Valley and the temple, Jesus gave, fulfilled, and *will* fulfill prophesy. From the Mount of Olives, Jesus made His triumphant entry into Jerusalem. It was here that Jesus gave His Olivet Discourse, predicting the destruction coming upon Jerusalem and the signs of the end of the age and the destruction yet to come upon the earth. It was here that Jesus spent hours agonizing in prayer the night before the cross in the Garden of Gethsemane and where He was arrested early that morning. From here, Jesus ascended into heaven, and here He will one day return. And it was here that we took turns reading Matthew, Chapter 24. The theme was **PROPHECY**.

At the Garden of Gethsemane, meaning "olive press," we read Luke 22:39-44. On the evening before Jesus' crucifixion, He prayed with overwhelming agony and sorrow, "Father, if you are willing, take this cup from me; yet not my will, but yours be done." The theme here was ***SURRENDER***.

King Hezekiah built Hezekiah's tunnel. It is a tunnel cut in the rock underneath the City of David, and it helped Jerusalem survive the siege of King Sennacherib of Assyria in 721 BC. It leads water from Gihon Spring to the Siloam Pool. The water from Gihon Spring is still the same water that flowed through it in biblical days. The tunnel is mentioned in 2 Chronicles 32:30.

Like the lyrics from Loch Lomond, "You'll take the high road, and I'll take the low road," we chose between the wet and dry side of Hezekiah's Tunnel. Please have your flashlight and water shoes ready as you descend into darkness and waist-deep water if you select the wet side. Depending on how busy it is, it can take up to forty minutes to walk through the 1720-foot-long tunnel. The second tunnel is dry, and it takes about 15 minutes to walk through—an exciting adventure either way.

As I stood at the Pool of Siloam where Jesus miraculously cured a man who was blind from birth, I thought back on when I was in elementary school. An optometrist told my mom and dad that my eyes were deteriorating at the rate of an older adult, and I was going blind. I knew something was very wrong when my mom told me to pick out anything I wanted in the Easter candy aisle and started crying. Years later, she shared with me how she had started fasting and praying at that time and how she had seen my father outside in the backyard praying for the Lord to take his eyes and not mine. When my mom, dad, and I went to the ophthalmologist, we received our miracle. The ophthalmologist told my parents that he saw no signs of any abnormalities in my eyes.

In Bethlehem and the neighboring Shepherds' Field, we took turns reading Luke 2:1-20. It was near here that Jacob buried Rachel. The theme was ***LOVE***. I hope you know how much God loves you!

The Eastern Gate is located in the Old City of Jerusalem on the opposite side of the Mount of Olives across from the Kidron Valley. It is the oldest of eight gates within the wall that surrounds the Old City of Jerusalem. The Eastern Gate is also called the Beautiful Gate and is completely sealed with sixteen feet of cement. It has been sealed for over 500 years. If you could walk through it, you would be very close to where the Jewish temple used to stand.

The Eastern Gate is believed to have been sealed to keep the Jewish Messiah from entering Jerusalem. Jewish heritage believes that the Messiah will pass through the Eastern Gate when He returns. The Muslim Suleiman attempted to foil the Messiah's plans with sixteen feet of cement.

On the southern steps of the temple area, where some of the original steps remain, we had my favorite teaching. We took turns reading John 7:2-37. When people come in contact with us as Christians, it is not us. It is the Holy Spirit. The Holy Spirit fills us up and overflows us. We become a source of refreshment for others, a sort of spiritual drinking fountain. The theme here was the ***OVERFLOW OF THE HOLY SPIRIT***. The overflow of the Holy Spirit is only found in a personal relationship with Jesus Christ.

View of Jerusalem from the Southern Steps

He was a lamb without spot or blemish. At the Praetorium, where Roman soldiers dressed
Jesus in a scarlet robe and twisted together a crown of thorns and placed it upon His head, we
took turns reading Mark, Chapter 15. Here Jesus was spat on, mocked, and flogged before
His crucifixion. The theme was *EXAMINATION*.

For those who trusted me with their prayer requests, they were delivered as high as I could reach into the crevasses of the Wailing Wall.

"To them, I will give within my temple and its walls a memorial and a name better than sons and daughters; I will give them an everlasting name that will endure forever." - Isaiah 56:5 Yad Vashem, Israel's memorial to the Jewish victims of the Holocaust.

"Remember only that I was innocent and, just like you, mortal on that day. I, too, had a face marked by rage, by pity and joy, quite simply, a human face." – Benjamin Fondane, Exodus, Murdered at Auschwitz, 1944.

As you enter the darkness of the children's memorial at Yad Vashem, you are overtaken by the reflection of candles that create the impression of a million stars shining. The carnage sinks in as 1.5 million murdered Jewish children's names, ages, and the country they were from is heard in the background. Never forget.

At the Garden Tomb, we took turns reading John, Chapter 19, and Isaiah, Chapter 53. As we shared communion, we shared what we think of when we take communion. I always ask God to make me as white as snow. "Come now, let us reason together, says the Lord: though your sins are like scarlet, they shall be as white as snow; though they are red like crimson, they shall become like wool." Isaiah 1:18 The theme here was *SALVATION*. If he had not walked His walk, I would not be walking mine.

The Pool of Bethesda, meaning "House of Grace," was a spring-fed pool with five porches. Invalids waited on the porches for a turn to step into the healing waters. It was here that Jesus healed a man who had been sick for thirty-eight years. We took turns reading John 5:2-15. The theme was **HOLINESS**. God does not heal us to return to our old, sinful life. The blessed, whole, safe life He provides us with is worth protecting.

The Valley of Elah was the site of David's slaying of the Philistine giant named Goliath. You may remember the story. Here we took turns reading 1 Samuel 17:2-58, and we were encouraged to collect five smooth stones just as David had done. The theme was ***UPLOOK***. When the outlook is dire, try the Uplook. "Our Father, which art in heaven, hallowed be thy name; thy kingdom come; thy will be done on earth as it is in heaven. Give us this day our daily bread; forgive us our trespasses as we forgive those who trespass against us; lead us not into temptation but deliver us from evil. For thine is the kingdom, the power, and the glory, forever and ever. Amen." is a wonderful way to start each day and an excellent reminder that there is a God above all of our circumstances.

In the Valley of Sorek, we took turns reading Judges, Chapter 16. Sin blinds us, binds us, and then grinds us. It was here that Samson fell in love with Delilah. She finally goads Samson into telling her that the secret behind his great strength is his hair, which she, in turn, reveals to the rulers of the Philistines. Both Delilah and Judas were paid in pieces of silver for their betrayal. As she lulls him to sleep on her lap, she calls for someone to shave his head. When she awakens him with a warning that the Philistines are upon him, he thinks he can go out and shake himself free as before. He did not know that the Lord had left him. The theme here was **SECOND CHANCES**. God is always willing to give us another chance.

In Joppa, Jonah tried to escape God's call upon his life, resulting in that well-remembered voyage. As we sat on steps overlooking the Mediterranean Sea, we took turns reading Acts, Chapter 10, remembering that not everyone has the same advantages we have. The theme was **GRACE**. We shouldn't judge others by our own experiences. God gives us grace, "For God so loved the world that He gave His one and only son, that whoever believes in Him shall not perish but have eternal life." - John 3:16, and we need to extend that same grace to others.

Walking through Joppa

One of my favorite keepsakes from Israel is a tear bottle. The small, glass vials were filled with the owner's tears and placed at the grave of their loved ones. Many tear bottles have been found when ancient tombs have been opened. Collecting tears in a bottle is mentioned in Psalm 56:8 when David prays to God, "You keep track of all my sorrows. You have collected all my tears in your bottle. You have recorded each one in your book." David's words remind us that God keeps a record of our pain. God did not forget David's sorrows, and He will not forget ours.

Walking down the Via Dolorosa, meaning "sorrowful road" in Latin, was Jesus' route from Pilate's judgment hall to Golgotha to be crucified. Picture the crowd pressing in to get a glimpse of His bloodied, beaten body, and never forget that He chose to take this road because of His love for you and me.

I had the pleasure of meeting Vic. He is the owner of Vic's Art Studio, Armenian Ceramics. His son runs the store when he travels to art exhibitions in Los Angeles, California. I bought one of his beautiful black and white pieces, and although no photography is allowed in the store, he let me take lots of pictures. Someone even took one of the two of us together. It was a great day!

Jesus was baptized in the Jordan River by John the Baptist and the Israelites had to cross it to enter the Promised Land. After the trip, Annie and I shared that being baptized in the Jordan River by Pastor Damian Kyle of Calvary Chapel, Modesto, in the name of the Father, the Son, and the Holy Spirit was the highlight of both of our trips.

Jordan River

"*To believe in Jesus* is to have a confident conviction that He is who the Bible says He is, He will keep His promises, and upon placing your trust in Him, you are entering into a personal, eternal relationship with the Son of God." – Charles Stanley

Do you believe? Your very life and afterlife depend on the answer to that question.

If you have placed your trust in Jesus Christ, congratulations! If not, do you want to begin a relationship with Him today?

"Behold, I stand at the door and knock. If anyone hears My voice and opens the door, I will come in..." Revelation 3:20

If your answer is yes, all you have to do is pray this prayer and mean it with your whole heart:

Dear God, as You stand at the door and knock, I open my heart to You. I realize I am less than perfect (a sinner). I ask You to forgive me of my sins. I believe You sent Your only Son to die in my place for my sins. Make me who I am supposed to be in Jesus Christ. I thank You for coming into my life and for saving me. In Jesus' name. Amen.

Pastor Damian

Pastor Damian Kyle, Senior Pastor
Calvary Chapel, Modesto, CA